Holiness in the Marketplace

Holiness in the Marketplace

by
Gene Van Note

BEACON HILL PRESS OF KANSAS CITY
Kansas City, Missouri

Copyright 1981
Beacon Hill Press of Kansas City

ISBN: 0-8341-0737-6

Printed in the
United States of America

Permission to quote from *The Holy Bible, New International Version* (NIV), copyright © 1978, by New York International Bible Society, is acknowledged with appreciation.

To my parents
with love

Contents

Preface	9
1. The Good Old Days	11
2. The Power of a Wish	18
3. Regardless of the Cost	28
4. Beauty for Ashes	36
5. Three Hours and Seven Miles Later	43
6. The Unplanned Response to a Crisis	49
7. Could a Man Ask for More?	58
8. Free to Love Again	67
9. Little Arnoldo	74
A Final Thought	83

Preface

Most people won't read this.

After all, what do you find in a preface—except names? And names are not important, unless one of them is yours. That means that you will not likely read much farther than the period at the end of this sentence.

But either now or later, I really do hope that you will carefully read the long list of names in this preface—not to see if you are here; you probably aren't. But to say, "Thank you!"

If there is anything in this book that brings a smile to your face, a tear to your eye, or prompts you to believe that there is hope in the future—for you, then you need to express your appreciation to these people. It is their book. They have helped me look through a window at a small portion of the lives of some unique followers of Christ.

So, since you have read this far, express your gratitude along with me for all these people who, through their courtesy, have made this book possible: Jerry Baker, Jorge de Barros, Clayton Bonar, Lawrence Bone, Tommy Burton, Steve Cooley, Jim Cummings, Alex R. G. Deasley, Leon Doane, Albert Garrick, Robert Goslaw, Anne Hamilton, Jack Hawthorne, Ross Hayslip, Harlan Heap, Harlan Heinmiller, James Hudson, Raymond Hurn, Clarence Jacobs, J. Dennis Johnson, Jerald D. Johnson, Jon Johnston, Earl Lee, Howard Mosley, Charles Muxworthy, Merritt Nielson, Ark Noel, John Oster, Kenneth Rice, Mel Rich,

Eugene Sanders, Robert Scott, M. V. "Bud" Scutt, Paul Simpson, Gilbertson Stuart, Bill Sullivan, William Taylor, William Vaughters, Melt Wienecke, John Williamson, and Floyd Young.

Oh yes, one more thing: The next time you greet any of these people, please tell them, "Thank you," for their contribution to this book.

1
The Good Old Days

> *O Lord, give me a backbone as big as a saw log; and ribs like the sleepers under the church floor; put iron shoes on me, and galvanized breeches. And give me a rhinoceros hide for a skin, and hang a wagonload of determination up in the gable end of my soul, and help me to sign a contract to fight the devil as long as I've got a tooth, and then gum him till I die. All this I ask for Christ's sake, Amen.*

These words of action and assurance come from a pioneer holiness evangelist, Rev. Reuben A. Robinson. However, no one ever knew him by that name. He was Rev. Bud Robinson to his early contemporaries, and "Uncle Buddy" to the thousands who heard him in later years. His "Daily Prayer," noted above, is an exhibit of the rugged dedication that characterized his commitment to the cause of Christ. He and countless men and women like him, both lay and clergy, lit the spark that eventually burst into flame as the Church of the Nazarene.

But it was not easy. Their allegiance to the holiness movement was costly in human relationships and personal advancement. They literally went out under the stars to preach the gospel of full salvation. The persecution that did not follow them was waiting for them to arrive.

Many people joined this new crusade, knowing full well what it would cost them. For example, on December 6, 1897, three farmers rented an empty store building in Sunset, Tex., for holiness services with some visiting evangelists. Though it had only straight plank seats with no backrests, the people crowded the hall to overflowing twice daily. The revival meeting lasted for three weeks with scores finding the Lord, and many experiencing God's grace in entire sanctification.

One of the seekers was Nettie, the popular daughter of a prominent businessman whose wife was a leader in local society. The family was humiliated when Nettie not only testified that she had been sanctified but also announced that she was called to preach.

Oscar Hudson, in *This I Remember*, recounts that Nettie's father said to her:

> "Nettie, this matter has gone too far. We are embarrassed when we appear in public, and you must give it up or I will have to disinherit you and ask you to leave home. I will give you 24 hours to make your decision."
>
> At the end of that time he entered her room and asked for her decision. With eyes swollen from weeping she placed her arms around his neck and said, "Daddy, I love you better than I love my life, but I love Jesus more."
>
> He asked, "Does that mean that you will not give up this nonsense?"
>
> She replied, "I can't."
>
> "Then," he said, "there is the door. Walk out and do not come back."

Later, at a nearby tent meeting, she rose from the altar with this shout:

> "Good-by society! Good-by loved ones! Good-by the church I love so well! If I can just live so that Jesus is

> not ashamed of me, it will be worth all the world beside." [Hudson, 16-17]

Utimately she was reconciled with her family, but she did not know it would ever happen when she made her decision.

It is easy to see how people who valued dignity and decorum above most everything else could easily have been offended by those pioneer "holiness folks."

In her autobiography, Mary Lee Cagle gives this account of a happening that was not uncommon in the early days.

> Another man, Grandpa Bales by name, was seventy years old, weighed two hundred pounds, with hair and beard as white as snow. He had rheumatism in his knees until he could hardly walk at times, but when the Spirit of God would come on him he would leap and jump, two or three feet high, and the power would fall on the entire audience. At first the mothers would hastily get their sleeping children up out of the straw, but they soon learned that there was no danger when Grandpa jumped, for he never hurt himself nor anyone else. He usually carried candy in his coat pockets for the children; one day he got blest and went leaping and as he would come down, the candy would jump out of his pockets; the children ran after him to pick up the candy. It was laughable. [Cagle, 68]

Mary Cagle herself is a compelling illustration of the dedication of those early leaders. The fact that she did not have the opportunity for much education did not thwart her from following the call of God. What she lacked in formal education she made up for in intensity. Her first husband died of tuberculosis, and she had a lifelong vulnerability to consumptive diseases especially when she was exhausted.

This episode from her autobiography is typical of the way she chose to live. Mary Cagle writes about herself in the third person in these words:

> She [Mary Cagle] was at Brother Sheeks' several days and was real sick all the time. The time came on now when she was to begin a meeting at Gladsen; but she was unable to go. She called in some of the saints and was anointed and prayed for healing and was wonderfully helped, but was not definitely healed. Some of the other workers went and started the meeting. She joined them in a few days but came very near fainting when she got off the train. Up to this time, she had taken no medicine; but here her friends persuaded her to have a doctor, which she did. She had no more chills, but was in a fearfully run-down condition, and, it seemed was right on the verge of tuberculosis or Bright's disease.
>
> The people kept asking for her to preach. One man said he would bring his office chair for her to sit in and preach. She said, "If I can preach at all, I can stand up." So they lifted her into a buggy, took her to the tent, helped her on the platform (she was so weak she had to hold the pulpit to stand in order to read her text); but when she began to speak God began to bless and the power of the Spirit came upon her and she preached with as much strength as she ever did and was heard a mile away. One woman said when she began, she asked the Lord to bless and keep her and give her strength; but she got to where she could only say, "Lord, keep her from killing herself if You can." [Cagle, 59]

Very little would have been accomplished without that level of commitment. Men and women literally burned themselves out in the cause of spreading scriptural holiness across the land.

Scriptural holiness was both a battleground and a battle cry. It signaled a degree of spiritual victory they had never experienced before. Widespread opposition to their discovery only increased the intensity of their devotion to what became known as the holiness movement. The Bible took on new life for these early believers. This was coupled with a new energy in their relationship with the Lord. Their preaching and teaching highlighted the biblical promise of full atonement; that promise included forgiveness for sins committed, cleansing from the nature of sin, and perfection in holy love.

Opportunities for discouragement came often. And when they came, the devil was always nearby to make certain these pioneers remembered that there was "an easier way." One Christmas morning, long before daylight lighted the west Texas plains, Mary Cagle was wrapped in a bed quilt, seated in the back of a bouncing wagon. Her hosts were a Swedish family who, though they hardly knew her, had invited Mary to spend the holiday season with them. She was separated from her family and on the way to a dawn Christmas service to be conducted in a language she did not understand.

The bitterly cold wind tore at the corners of the ragged blanket while her archenemy tore at the corners of her spirit. Satan sat beside her on that board plank and said accusingly, "Now, aren't you making a fool of yourself, out here this time of night in the cold. You know it will make you sick."

Her response was characteristic: "That may all be so, but the dear Lord knows that there is not enough money in Texas to hire me to do this, but for His sake and the sake of souls, I will gladly do it." [Cagle, 44]

Human memory is highly selective. It tends to bring into consciousness those experiences of either pain or pleasure that support what we want to believe or promote in the present. Thus, the selection of early events usually centers either on the depth of commitment or the size of the victory achieved by the pioneers.

But not every sermon convinced sinners they needed to be saved. Believers were not always sanctified. Some pastors quit because it was too tough. Laymen were known to return to their sinful habits and dishonest business practices. Churches were born. Some lived, some died.

Yet the work went on. It was carried on the shoulders of men like Rev. Claude Robinson, who reported at the yearly holiness meeting that it had been a hard year—only one person had decided to follow Christ. Yet he rejoiced because he had succeeded in winning that one soul to Jesus "and expressed himself as being willing to work another whole year to win one more soul." [Cagle, 90]

However, these are not "the good old days." Incredible changes have taken place since Nettie decided to become a believer in the last month of 1897. These changes have had a powerful impact on the church. No longer are worshippers forced to defend against the cold with a tattered blanket as they cross the desolate prairie on the way to church. Our temperature-controlled cars are more comfortable than even the finest homes were in those days.

But not everything has changed.

The gospel message is still being preached. Sinners are being converted; believers are entering into the experience of entire sanctification; men and women are still making the unswerving commitment to follow Christ regardless where His will might take them. For some, as in earlier days, that decision is costly in human relationships and personal advancement. But there has been no retreat. As has been said so well, "They not only counted the cost, they discounted the cost."

This is a book about some of those people, the kind who have gone counter to the selfish greed of our day. They are real people, all of whom were living when this book went to press.

These believers have come to grips with some formidable challenges and have come through victoriously. This does not mean that they have never had to face another problem. In fact, right now they may be struggling with difficulties greater than these. But at these points they have been successful. We do not worship them, but we do salute them and walk in the path they have lighted by their devotion. They have demonstrated that the sanctified life is not reserved for "super Christians" secluded in cloistered halls. They have proven that the reverse is true. Holiness can be lived in the marketplace.

2
The Power of a Wish

The young harbor pilot left home with great reluctance that morning. Soon his wife would give birth to their firstborn, but he could not stay. A messenger had just arrived with the information that a schooner needed to be guided into port. As he left, he gave specific instructions to the midwife. When his wife had delivered, if mother and baby were both doing well, she was to go to the front of their beachside home and wave a large white cloth. He would respond by waving a white flag to acknowledge the receipt of the message.

The harbor pilot was pleasantly surprised when he climbed on board the schooner. The captain was a boyhood friend from the little village in Italy where they had spent their childhood. As they worked their way into the harbor at Fuena on the island of Brava in the Cape Verde Islands, the pilot shared with his friend what was taking place at home.

"Then you do your job," the schooner captain told him, "and I'll watch for the flag.

"There it is," the captain finally shouted; "I'll bet it's a girl!"

As soon as the ship was docked, the harbor pilot rushed home, the captain following in his wake. The captain's guess was correct. The proud parents named their new daughter Adelina.

This is the story of Mrs. Adelina Domingues, born 95 years ago on Brava, one of the smallest and most often drouth-stricken islands in the Cape Verde chain.

Within two hours of Adelina's birth the schooner captain placed an expensive gold earring in her left hand while her father folded her right hand around the gold coin he had just earned. Then the captain continued, "Let me make a wish for her future. I wish that when this girl grows up, she will be as pure as gold."

Because of their religious background, neither of them knew how to pray. This was their expression of hope for Adelina. That wish was to have a tremendous impact on her as she grew older.

Adelina was still a child when they pierced her ear and inserted the earring. Her earliest memories are of listening to her mother tell about the schooner captain's wish. Very early in life she decided, "I'm going to do all I can to be what that man wants me to be."

In those days, all of the residents of Brava were Roman Catholics. They lived under the pressure of the priests who controlled them with the threat of an extended time in purgatory.

Adelina had a tender conscience coupled with a sincere religious spirit. As a young Roman Catholic she lived as clean as she knew how. She recalls, "I did nothing to displease God. I lived the best I knew under the Roman Catholic law. I was very religious."

Whatever the priest suggested, she did. One day, when Adelina was in her mid-teens, the priest told her, "The only 'wrong' in you is original sin. You'll have to go to purgatory, but you'll not have to stay long there because you are so good."

However, the rituals and ceremonies of her Roman Catholic faith did not satisfy her hunger for real meaning in religious worship. As a teenager, she would go down into the valley, crawl under the low-hanging branches of a coffee tree, and pray: *God, my mother tells me that You are in heaven, but that You are in the earth, too. Would You send an angel and tell me what to do so I can be forgiven and not have to go to purgatory?*

But the angel never came!

When Adelina was 19 years of age, her father asked her to walk to the northern part of the island to pay a man for a horse saddle. Near her destination she stopped at a home to ask for directions. Neither she nor the man who answered her knock realized that within 30 days he would become her father-in-law.

Three days after that chance meeting, the two fathers arranged the marriage between Jose Manuel Domingues and Adelina. But she was the last to know that she was going to be married!

At this point, a bit of Jose's background is important to understand the story. The son of well-to-do parents, Jose had run away from home to become a mess-boy on a whaler. At a stop-over in Florida some young ladies from Bethel Mission gave Jose a Bible and a New Testament in Portuguese, his native language.

A few weeks later when the whaler made port at Providence, R.I., Jose met three young Cape Verdians who invited him to church. There, at the South Providence Church of the Nazarene, he heard the story of salvation for the first time. He accepted God's grace and became a follower of the Lord Jesus Christ. Shortly thereafter, the four Cape Verdian boys decided to return home "to tell our families about the Bible."

The families of three of the boys responded with joy. Jose's family was different. Fanatic Roman Catholics, they resisted angrily, rejected his testimony, and started a campaign of persecution to destroy his new faith. The men held him down, poured whiskey on his head and in his mouth. But he would not swallow it, and thus they could not get him drunk.

Unsuccessful, they tried another tactic. They provided him with lots of money and access to many girls of questionable morality. It worked. He was unable to control his youthful passions and not only backslid, but he was launched on a lifetime of immorality—a life-style that marriage did not change.

Several years later, after Jose had qualified for his ship captain's license, Adelina went one day to pay a man for a horse's saddle.

Thirty days later they were married. Following local custom she moved into the home of her in-laws. A Roman Catholic neighbor had given her instructions for her wedding night—instructions that she intended to follow every night after that also. She had been assured that this would keep her marriage from failing.

As soon as she and Jose were alone, she went to each of the four corners of the room and made the sign of the Cross. Then she repeated a prayer to the Virgin Mary, after which she prayed the rosary.

Jose looked on with a bit of a smile on his face. Finally, he said quietly, "I feel sorry for you. But you're young; you have time to learn."

A few days later, Jose was scheduled to leave for the United States as the captain of a small schooner. On the night before he left, Jose told Adelina: "The thing that bothers me most about you is your religion. You are a fanatic. Did you ever read the Bible?"

"Oh, no!" Adelina reacted. "There is no Bible here; and besides, we are not allowed to read the Bible. The priest says that if we read the Bible, we will have to live more than 100 years in purgatory."

"Ada," he said gently, "there's no purgatory. Did the priest ever tell you why Jesus died on the Cross?"

"No, the priest never told us. Maybe He wanted to make religious medals for us."

Jose continued, "God is good and doesn't lie. The Bible opens your heart like a letter. In the Bible you read about how Christ died for you. He paid for your salvation."

"No," Adelina replied, "you have to go to purgatory to pay for your sins before you can go to heaven."

"If you have a bill and I pay it, what would you think if someone demanded that you pay it again?"

"I would think that he is a thief."

"Ada, God has paid for your redemption. He is not a thief. He won't charge you twice."

Thus her backslidden husband gave her the first instruction in the way of salvation. His closing advice was: "Read the Bible and see what God wants you to be."

"But, Jose, I don't have a Bible."

"I know where one is," he replied. Then he went to his parents' bedroom, without their knowledge, and brought back the Bible and New Testament they had taken from him seven years earlier. His mother had hidden it in a chest. As Jose gave it to his new bride, he told her, "Ada, I must go to America tomorrow. In order to get there, I must have a map. To get to heaven, you must have a map. Here, take this and read it every day. Do not let anyone know you have it. Do what it says and take Jesus as the Captain of your ship."

"Are you a Protestant, Jose?"

"I used to be a Christian until I went to eat with the pigs."

"You don't look like a pig," Adelina responded playfully. "Do you eat with the pigs?"

"I am not a four-foot pig, I am a two-foot pig. We are all two-foot pigs until we are cleansed by God."

The next morning Adelina climbed as high up on the mountain as she could so she could watch her husband's ship as far out into the sea as possible. When his schooner had disappeared, she was alone with her thoughts. She remembers, "I began to feel something touching my heart. I began to feel that there was a possibility that there is a God. I began to get hungry to read the Bible."

That night after everyone had gone to sleep, Adelina picked up the Bible. With trembling hands she held the Holy Book for a long time. Finally, encouraged by the words of her husband, she let the Bible fall open.

Surely it was not an accident that it opened at the third chapter of John—the story of Nicodemus. Adelina said, almost out loud, as she read, "Here is a man who didn't know God either." She continued to read.

Finally she asked herself, "How can I know how to be born of the Spirit, if there is no one to tell me?" To her mind this answer came: To be born of the Spirit is to have a brand-new beginning. Just like a baby is born, the Holy Spirit will be a mother to you. You are going to begin a new life. Your sin is paid.

Suddenly something happened! "I felt a joy I cannot express! I fell down on my knees on the bed and started to talk with God. *You have come into my heart,* I prayed. *I am going to start a new life.*"

The transformation brought such great joy that she was filled with laughter. But in her excitement she lost her place in the Bible. So she said to herself, "I know how to pray now. I am going to ask God to open the Bible to that place for me." Having prayed, she opened the Bible; but instead, a new passage came to her eyes: "If any man will come after me, let him deny himself, and take up his cross, and follow me" (Matt. 16:24).

She thought again of the child, and how it needed food. Then it seemed she heard the Lord impress her: *You are clean, but you need the Holy Spirit in your life. He will be your Strength, your Guide. He will never leave you. . . . Are you willing to deny father, mother, church, and friends?*

She replied, *Yes.*

Then she remembers, "I was filled with joy. I felt strong enough to kill a lion!"

Sometime past midnight she asked, *Lord, what do You want me to do?"*

I want you to carry My name to the poorest people—to love them for Me—this is your lifetime job.

Some years later, not long after she had emigrated to the U.S. with her husband, Adelina started out one Sunday morning to find a church. She asked a man, standing on a corner in New Bedford, Mass., "Where is a good church—people who enjoy their religion?"

He directed Adelina to a small church a few blocks away. The sign on the front read, "Church of the Nazarene." There she made many new friends and discovered a doctrinal explanation for the saving and sanctifying grace she had experienced much earlier at home on the island of Brava.

Adelina Domingues became a vital part of the New Bedford church. Across the years her reputation grew as a woman of faith and prayer, dynamic and courageous. Nor did she lose her compassion for the poor. For many years she tried to involve the local Cape Verdians in her church. But for various reasons, they did not feel welcome. Out of that tension has come the International Church of the Nazarene in New Bedford. To simply say that she played a significant role in its current success is to overlook the obvious and underplay the years of hard work. From its humble beginning as the Free-Gospel Mission to its current place of effective ministry, God has blessed this church. A host of people will meet Adelina in heaven and say, "Thank you!"

"95 Jenny Street, New Bedford, Mass., stands out in my memory as the scene of one of the great all-time experiences in my life," writes Earl Mosteller, missionary to Portugal. Earl and his wife spent 15 months living upstairs in Adelina's home near the end of World War II. From her they learned how to speak the Portuguese language and to appreciate the Cape Verdian culture. She provided them an invaluable introduction for their years of successful missionary work on the Cápe Verdian Islands.

The Mostellers write these memories:

During our second term of service in the Cape Verde Islands, Mrs. Domingues, known as Doña Adelina, visited her native island, Brava. Although she was at least 65 years old, and traveling in sailboats, on donkeys, etc. wasn't easy, we felt that her contagious Christian spirit was something that the other islands should share. So we invited her to tour with us. Men of position listened in amazement. Great and small heard her talk about Jesus Christ. There were no barren altars after her testimonies.

We were stunned one morning when one of our main pastors came to us and said he was quitting. He had been sorely tried and felt he was the victim of injustice. We called Mrs. Dominques to pray for him. As she started to pray, she began to tell how Christ had suffered, how He had been unjustly treated, how He had been rejected. By this time the tears were flowing down her cheeks and her voice was rising in a crescendo of pathos until we were feeling a little of the suffering Christ.

As a direct result of her prayer, the pastor took on new courage and returned to his assignment. Eventually he served some of the largest Cape Verdian churches and became one of the most effective district superintendents on that island district.

Jose Domingues was responsible for the conversion of his wife, Adelina. In those early days he was active with Rev. John Diaz in the beginnings of the Church of the Nazarene in Cape Verde. But under pressure he lost his way. His wife prayed for his conversion throughout his life. One day it seemed to Adelina that the Lord commanded her, *Take your hands off; let Me handle your husband.*

She replied, *I'll never pray for him again.* Three weeks later, Jose became desperately sick. He got only as far as the hospital in Wollaston, Mass., on the way home.

Adelina went to see him. They talked about their long life together. Faced with an uncertain future, he became quite repentant. She assured him of her continued love and reminded him that forgetfulness goes with forgiveness.

Yet he could not believe that after his long life of sin God still loved him. Faith was reborn when Adelina asked, "Do you think I've got more love in my heart than God?"

Three weeks before he died, Jose found his way back to the Savior of his youth. His comment about his wife stands as the greatest tribute she has ever received: "I've never met anyone with so much love!" It is a love that the passing years have not diminished. Adelina Domingues demonstrates the truth of the ancient hymn:

Fear not; I am with thee. Oh, be not dismayed,
For I am thy God, I will still give thee aid.
I'll strengthen thee, help thee, and cause thee to stand,
Upheld by My gracious, omnipotent hand."

Mrs. Domingues was born, and grew to maturity, in a culture that did not grant a woman very many civil or domestic rights. Even after she emigrated to "the land of the free," she was the prisoner of those ancient customs. Her domineering husband resisted all her attempts to help others through the Protestant church. Yet, in spite of these handicaps, she found creative ways to express her holy love for her poor countrymen adrift in a new and lonely world.

In the next chapter we will meet a man who has walked the corridors of power. As a close political associate of a man who later became president of the United States, he faced a unique challenge—one that does not come to many Christians.

3

Regardless of the Cost

Almost nothing takes place in a vacuum. An occasional scientific experiment may, but not life. Life is people—the daily interaction with other human beings. For the most part, the quality and the morality of life is judged in relation to people also. In fact, except for the recluse, the actions and reactions of human experience can only be understood in the context of daily living.

Decisions, even the big choices, do not stand alone. It may well be that what seem, to the outsider, to be life-shaping decisions are not that at all. They arrive at the end of a long string of choices, each contributing to the moral fiber that makes a major decision actually only the expected result of a predetermined life-style.

This is the simple explanation of what happened in the life of Alex Steinkamp. It took place one Sacramento morning when he was selected to be the deputy state treasurer for the state of California. It was a position he held for eight years while Ronald Reagan was governor and Ivy Baker Priest was treasurer of the Golden State.

It is easier to understand the conversation that took place in Alex's office between him and Mrs. Priest after you have had a chance to get acquainted with him.

Alex was just a boy in the Junior Department in Sunday School when his family moved to Sacramento. Devout Christians, his parents became active members of the Church of the Nazarene in the capital city. Now known as the First Church of the Nazarene, it was a happy, spirited group in those early days. They possessed faith and vision coupled with a compelling mission to bring scriptural holiness to that key city in California's great inland valley.

During the late 1920s, their success in evangelism had crowded out their worship facilities. Thus, with great optimism, they launched a building program to construct a new sanctuary and attendant Sunday School rooms. Times were good; money was plentiful; jobs were easy to find; and building loans were readily available.

First Church borrowed the money they needed to bring the project to completion. By modern standards, the loan was a paltry sum. But by contemporary standards the payments would test the mettle of the congregation, at least for the first few years while the membership continued to grow.

Then, almost without warning, the United States economy went sour. The members of First Church were not exempt from the brutal impact of the Great Depression. Men who thought they had comfortable security on their jobs were laid off. Many who continued to be employed were forced to take a severe cut in pay.

And with it, contributions to the support of the church also fell alarmingly. A year or two earlier the mortgage had seemed to be a major challenge. Now it was an impossible obstacle.

During the next few years, every church in Sacramento, representing all denominations, settled with their creditors for a fraction of their financial obligation. Banks holding church mortgages arranged the best deal they could—often for as low as 25 cents on the dollar. Not a church in Sacramento paid off their loans in full.

Except one: the First Church of the Nazarene. The members decided that they would not "cheat" anyone because of their lack of foresight. They would make every payment, honor every commitment.

That was a stiff price to pay when there were attractive options. Other churches were defaulting; they could too! Their choice was costly. The members made unbelievable sacrifices: They double- and triple-tithed; some took second mortgages on their homes; more moved down from fine cars to rattletraps; some ladies sold their furs and gave the money to help make the mortgage payments.

It was not easy.

But it did not go unnoticed. The Sacramento financial community became aware of their valiant effort. Every banker in the city knew what was happening. It is an interesting sidelight to the story to note that bankers have long memories. A quarter century later, following World War II, the U.S. was enjoying a pleasant financial climate. The horrors of the depression were faded memories. A small home mission church, that had been organized out of First Church, applied for a loan to purchase a parsonage. Their income was limited, and they could not have qualified on their own. However, the depression repayment record of First Church became their "cosigner," and they were granted the loan. The sacrifices of that congregation had a tremendous influence on the financiers of the capital city.

The sacrificial commitment "to do what was right regardless of the cost" also made an incredible impact on one of their young men. Alex Steinkamp has lived his life aware of both the glory and the personal consequences of that kind of decision. The adults, after whom he was molding his life, had provided a clear example of how to be happy while making the tough choice. The church members may have sacrificed, but never in the atmosphere of gloom and despair. They were delighted to be Christians, even with an old car and a second mortgage on their homes.

It was in that community of happy believers that Alex grew to adulthood and entered the world of finance. Prior to those difficult years, about 1925, he was hired by one of the better banks in Sacramento. It was an excellent place to work and the future seemed limitless. He decided to place his career and his life savings in their keeping.

Eight years later the bank closed—not for a day, but forever. It was insolvent. Alex lost everything. All of his dreams and hopes, as well as his savings account, were wrapped up in that financial institution.

Alex was only one of thousands of men looking for work in 1933. Thus, he did not have high hopes when he applied, along with a great many others, for a position in the state treasurer's office.

He took the exam—and waited. And waited. And waited.

Finally, when he had almost given up hope, he was notified that he had been hired. It was not much of a job. But it was a job. Alex was grateful for it, even though it was the most basic entry-level position, and the salary reflected its unimportance.

The job had at least one positive side benefit, however. The relative security of his new position gave him confidence to take a step he had looked forward to for some time. In 1934, Alex and a young lady named Olive were married. She and her family had moved to Sacramento shortly after the Steinkamps' arrival. Olive brought both a serenity and a conquering confidence to the relationship. Their life has been a happy partnership.

Olive remembers those early days: "Alex started at the very bottom in the treasurer's office—the lowest salary you could imagine—working his way up through unbelievable obstacles."

When asked to identify some of the obstacles her husband faced in the state treasurer's office, Olive observed, "The opposition to Alex came because of his religious convictions. You see," she continued, "his Christian stance really did hold him back. He didn't drink, he didn't smoke; and whenever he had a chance to tell someone about Jesus Christ, he wasn't afraid to witness."

Alex Steinkamp's future was further clouded by his political affiliation—he is a member of the Republican Party. Historically, most of the governors of the state of California have been Democrats.

Across the years, Alex watched as many men with far less seniority were promoted above him. On some occasions, they clearly were not nearly as capable as he. He became a ringside observer of the rules by which power politics were played. There were even a few times when Alex would not have been surprised if he had been fired because he chose to follow his Christian convictions rather than the politically attractive route.

In 1967, Ronald Reagan, currently the president of the United States, became the governor of the state of California. In the same election, Mrs. Ivy Baker Priest was chosen by the voters to be the state treasurer. Earlier she had been the treasurer of the United States during the administration of President Dwight Eisenhower.

At this time, Alex Steinkamp was working as an investment officer in the state treasurer's office. In retrospect, he notes that "during the many years I had worked in the state treasurer's office, when a new state treasurer was elected and came to the state capitol to assume the duties of the office, he or she always brought in a friend to be the deputy—usually one who was politically involved in the election."

Thus, Alex was more than a bit puzzled when, one morning, Mrs. Priest entered his office and sat down across the desk from him. After a few minutes of casual conversation, she said, "Mr. Steinkamp, I have decided that you are to be my deputy state treasurer."

Alex could hardly believe what he had heard. After so many years, he had concluded that he "had reached the top." Now he was being asked to become the second in command in the treasurer's office of one of the most prosperous states in the republic. In fact, only a very few nations in the world have a larger gross national product than California.

It was a position of power and influence—a dream come true when the dream had almost faded away.

However, there were more important things than the fulfillment of a dream. Alex had grown to manhood in a group that believed that they had to "do what was right regardless of the cost." Without asking for time to consider the attractive offer, Alex responded to Mrs. Priest.

After expressing his gratitude and surprise that he had been selected to be the deputy state treasurer, Alex added, "I don't know you, and I don't know Mr. Reagan. However, before you make a public announcement about my appointment, there is something you should know about me.

"I am a Christian. For many years now, I have attempted to live a careful Christian life, both in my home and business relationships.

"As you know, I have worked for the state for a long time. During much of that time I have been in a position to see what goes on behind the scenes. Nearly everyone I have worked with, both those above and those below me, have been very honest. There have been times, though, when political pressure has been exerted in an attempt to gain improper advantage through illegal or unethical methods. I do not want to put you or the governor in an embarrassing political situation. I don't know what might happen, but if I were asked to do something improper, I would refuse. That could cause problems for Mr. Reagan.

"Perhaps it would be better for all concerned if you would withdraw your kind offer."

Ivy Baker Priest replied, "That's exactly why I'm selecting you for this important position, Mr. Steinkamp. We probably know more about you than you know about yourself. Our investigators have probed into every aspect of your life—both public and private."

She told him that everyone at every level had spoken most highly of his professional expertise and his personal honesty. One leading executive in the Bank of America, California's largest statewide banking chain, testified, "The strongest he'll ever drink is tomato juice. You should never hesitate to appoint Alex Steinkamp—he is a man of integrity."

When the choice of Alex Steinkamp to be deputy treasurer was announced, he was asked, "Now what are you going to do with your life-style? You don't drink and you don't do these other things. What now?"

Alex simply replied, "I'm going to do just exactly what I've always done."

In retrospect, he adds that during Reagan's administration, "I was never asked to do anything that was contrary to my standards as a Christian."

Now retired from state service, Alex Steinkamp is a West Coast representative for a prestigious Wall Street investment firm. His Christian witness continues at the highest levels in the world of politics and finance.

A man's character, revealed in a moment of opportunity or challenge, is molded across thousands of days of unheralded, seemingly minor decisions. For that reason, it can be said with confidence that this humble man has lived a life of holiness in the marketplace.

For the devout follower of Christ, government service has some special challenges. Political advancement and holy living are, unfortunately, not always compatible.

People who serve their government in other ways face unique hazards, too. The career civil service employee, who is required to relocate often, is cut off from family and friends. This anonymous life has some enchanting temptations built into it. The unexpected impact of this life-style on one couple is the focus of the story in our next chapter.

4
Beauty for Ashes

Our tale begins in "Robber's Roost," Okla., a few years after the Indian Territory became a state in 1907. There, a perspiring country doctor delivered a tiny baby girl. She was the first of four daughters to be born to a young cowboy and his schoolteacher wife.

They named her Hilda. Her parents' friends knew them as Bill and Bessie Furlong.

Actually, Robber's Roost is as much a slice of history as a geographical location. In fact, even then you could not have found it on the map. It was only a small, remote log cabin—built and then deserted by a dry land farmer. However, it did not stay empty. It became a hideout for cattle rustlers and stagecoach robbers. A major trail over which cattle were driven from Kansas to Texas was nearby. It was rumored that an old Indian squaw lived in the cabin and welcomed the thieves as they came there to rest, water their horses, and divide their booty. Many men had been killed there, illustrating that there is not always "honor among thieves."

Incidentally, for the curious reader, the log cabin no longer exists but was located in south-central Oklahoma, near the present city of Durant.

It is a long way from Robber's Roost to Washington, D.C. Years later, in that capital city, Hilda Furlong's greatest crisis occurred. But there were places to go, sights to be seen—and half a life to be lived before the phone rang in her Arlington, Va., home, near the national Capitol.

A young navy man, whose family name was Moffitt, changed the direction of her life. Hilda met him after her family moved to San Diego. Following their marriage, they shared a call into the ministry. It was a six-year ministry of music that involved them in an active gospel quartet and a regular religious radio program. All this was possible after her husband was discharged from the service.

Then came an exciting opportunity for her husband to continue his government service in the Orient. The years flew by. Three children became a part of the family: Esther, Stephen, and Virginia. By the time the government transferred them to Washington, D.C., each of the children had married and had begun their own family.

Life in the Moffitt home was hectic during those days. Both Hilda and her husband had full-time jobs and interests outside the home. Their busy schedules, however, could not hide the fact that their relationship had begun to crack.

In early September, 1965, as the bright light of the full moon came beaming through the bedroom window, Hilda lay sobbing. Because of a painful confrontation with her husband, her body would not yield to the tiredness that engulfed her. His outside interests had taken him away from their mutual interest in the church. That vacancy in his life had been filled by an intimate involvement with his secretary.

Now that the tension of hiding an illicit relationship was released, he went to sleep. Not even his shattered wife's anguish disturbed him.

Then the phone rang: long distance from Las Vegas; person-to-person for Mr. Moffitt.

Hilda awakened him and watched with increasing fear as his expression changed abruptly. Full-flowing sentences were replaced by curt questions and brief comments.

Abruptly, he hung up the phone, refused to answer any questions, and left their apartment.

Three hours later he returned, walking like a man who had been drugged. All self-assurance was gone. Taking Hilda's hand as he sat on the edge of the bed, he said, with great effort, "Esther has just been told by her doctor that she has acute, terminal leukemia and is not expected to live more than three months, if that long."

Let's listen in as Hilda remembers the shock of that moment.

> Esther—my lovely blond, blue-eyed eldest daughter—only 29 years of age.
>
> We yielded to our grief. Both my husband and I wept unreservedly in each other's arms. When our tears were spent, my husband explained that Esther had felt that her message would be too painful for me and had asked her father to wait until later to tell me. When he had hung up the phone, he had gone downstairs to our son Steve's apartment. I was grateful that Steve counseled his father to inform me immediately.
>
> When the sun rose the next morning, after a few fitful hours of sleep, I had a double load to carry. Both my 29-year-old daughter and my 33-year-old marriage were dying.

Shortly after the phone call Esther's condition improved. The leukemia went into remission.

Four months later the Moffitts made an emergency flight to Las Vegas. Their younger daughter, Virginia, met them at the airport and took them directly to Sunrise Hospital. There, in a first-floor room, Esther lay in isolation.

The hospital gowns and sterile masks could not hide the emotions. "As we kissed her," Hilda recalls, "it was almost impossible to keep from weeping, for we were shocked at the change the dread disease had inflicted on our lovely daughter."

Days and nights seemed without end. Surface optimism and impending doom walked hand in hand.

Abruptly, Esther's condition improved. One sunny day when she was home and comfortable in her own bed, she confided in her mother that she wanted her to tell the children that she was going to die.

Each night, in her prayers, Hilda asked the Lord to help her find the words for this mission of sorrow. She remembered that Esther's first child, David, had died a few hours after birth—a fact that had been shared with the other children.

Hilda recalls how she broke the tragic news to her grandchildren:

> One evening, before I tucked them into bed, I decided it was time to reveal the seriousness of their mother's illness.
>
> I asked them, "Do you know what it means to die?"
>
> They confidently responded, "You don't live in your body anymore, but you live in heaven."
>
> I said, "Yes, that's right. Your little brother has been in heaven for a long time without his mother, and you have had her for several years. You know how very sick your mother has been lately. The doctors say that she has a disease that no known medicine can cure. In a short time now she will become a spirit and go join God and David and live with them forever in heaven. Even though it will make us sad and lonely, just think how happy David and your mother will be to be together again."
>
> Kelly asked, "Grandmother, will my mother be well and happy up there—will she be beautiful like she used to be?"

I squeezed the tears back and calmly answered, "She will be even more beautiful, and will always be healthy and happy."

Kelly's little sister, Robin, asked some questions. We talked for a long time and then they went quietly to sleep. From that night on they gave their mother even more loving attention. Their schoolwork improved, and they seemed to be experiencing the peace of God.

Other members of the family arrived shortly after that, allowing Hilda and her husband to return home. A few weeks later they received a phone call from Las Vegas. Esther had been set free from her prison of pain.

Kelly was the first person to greet Hilda when she disembarked from the airplane. He put his arms around her tightly and exclaimed, "Grandmother, guess what! Mother is a spirit now, just like you said she would be. She won't be sick anymore."

As I held him close, I knew that God's wisdom had been given as my grandchildren were prepared to face their mother's death with courage. I silently breathed my gratitude to God for His loving direction.

During the year that followed Esther's funeral, Hilda's marriage deteriorated rapidly. One day her husband abruptly informed her that he had quit his job with the government. Unable to find employment after searching for several weeks, he told Hilda that he was going to visit their children in California—alone. He suggested that when he returned, they would start a new life together.

Most of their lovely furniture was sold. Hilda moved into a small studio apartment. He shipped quite a few things he said they would use to "set up housekeeping in the West."

Seven weeks later, without warning, I received a divorce decree from a lawyer in Las Vegas, Nev. My ex-husband had made no provision for my future. I had been abandoned—34 years wiped away as if they were nothing. The devastation I felt I cannot describe. I had to face the fact that all my husband's planning for us to make a new start together had been a cruel deceit.

The storm outside my window had subsided a few hours after it began, but the storm in my heart continued to rage. A host of unfamiliar feelings flooded me day and night: fear of a future I felt incapable of facing alone; resentment at being robbed not only of the security of possessions and money, but of my husband whom I still loved; rage at the deceitfulness of it all.

Although I went to work each day facing the public as though nothing had happened, at night I fought the battle until my physical and emotional health were in peril. I had never before felt my prayers so ineffectual. Something had to be done.

About two o'clock one morning I awoke from a nightmare with my pillow wet from tears shed during a restless sleep. I knelt beside my bed crying to God for help. I'm sure He directed me to open my Bible to Isa. 61:3, for the beautiful promises in that scripture became real in a special way as I read, ". . . to give unto them beauty for ashes, the oil of joy for mourning, the garment of praise for the spirit of heaviness." God answered my prayer, making those promises personal to me. I felt the deep, healing touch of the Spirit of God and slept peacefully the rest of the night for the first time since the divorce notice came.

From the ashes of my burned-out marriage I began to build a new life alone. The first hurdles were to face and release the resentment of what my husband had done to me, and to change my wifely love to a forgiving Christian love. Though it took time and was not easy, God led me lovingly and gently into a forgiving spirit.

During the next few months I updated my secretarial skills by attending night school classes. It was important to qualify for a position that would pay enough to supply my financial needs. Though the job market is more favorable to youth, I obtained a fine job on the West Coast where I moved to live near my children and other family members.

As I grow older, coping alone is complex, for I still miss my companion of many years. The loneliness sometimes threatens to be overwhelming, but I draw on God's help for the strength and courage to go on joyfully. I live a busy life, and it is my privilege to often share my healing experience with other women who struggle with the aftereffects of divorce. It is a joy to encourage them to seek God's help in their own way.

I was forced without my consent to break my marriage vow, "Until death do us part," but the storm produced in my life by that break has been calmed by God's touch as He gave me beauty instead of fear, joy replacing sorrow, and praise each day for His protective and releasing love.

The ancient sufferer, Job, learned through his personal agony that righteousness is no barrier to sorrow. He was sustained by the conviction that he had done no wrong and that God was honorable and trustworthy. Faith was triumphant, though questions remained.

In our day, as Hilda Moffitt has illustrated, faith is enhanced by love—God's perfect love growing in the life of those who are completely committed to follow Him. And yet, even that love can be tested to the ultimate, as we shall see in the next chapter. The story of Jean Leathers Phillips is a beautiful expression of Christian joy in the midst of unbelievable heartache.

5

Three Hours and Seven Miles Later

Jean Leathers Phillips had had a distinguished career as a writer. She shares a vulnerability common to all writers. What was published in the past can be brought into the present to judge whether the writer can practice what she preaches.

For example, note this carefree poem printed in the *Herald of Holiness,* August 21, 1937:

> *Faith is like birds northward winging*
> *Above earth cloaked with snow,*
> *Like willow pussy kittens clinging*
> *While chill blasts fiercely blow.*

Another of her poems that appeared in the same magazine 17 years later shows that her lighthearted optimism was challenged by the harsh realities of life—challenged, but not shattered. Read:

"This thing will pass and all will be well tomorrow,"
  My comforters, well meaning, gently said
When on my heart was poured a cup of sorrow,
  And clouds of trial gathered 'round my head.

> *Then came my Father with strength unmeasured,*
> *With tender mercies, more than tongue can tell,*
> *And said: "My child, My dearly loved and treasured,*
> *I am with you and now are all things well."*

That "cup of sorrow" was filled to overflowing after years of heartache. The final episode came abruptly—"three hours and seven miles later," to recall the mother's anguished words. What happened at the end of those three hours and seven miles is our story. The poems reveal the depth of maturity gained in the "valley of the shadow," and the extent of her personal victory through suffering.

First, let's meet Jean Leathers Phillips.

Jean lives today in a small residential apartment in San Diego. When asked how she spends her time, she replied, "I'm not doing a lot right now; I'm 85. I've turned all the writing over to the younger people."

Well, almost all of it! Ten years ago she quit writing, having worn out her fourth typewriter since 1917. But her friends in San Diego First Church knew that she was not ready to quit. Without her knowledge they privately raised the money to purchase a new typewriter. From it numerous Christian articles have come. But now, even that part of her life is history. Presently in her 86th year, she carries on an active correspondence with 25 missionary families. She writes personal letters on the occasion of every important day—birthdays, anniversaries, holidays, etc.—several hundred letters a year. Each Sunday morning, just prior to the worship service, Jean "makes a sweep" through the Sunday School classrooms, collecting appropriate pieces of unused material for inclusion in her letters. The cost of postage is a significant item in her fixed budget, money that could profitably be used for personal expenses but is used in this fashion without complaint.

Jean Leathers Phillips began her writing career long before her marriage to a career army man in 1922. Prior to that time she was successful as a free-lance writer, and had also served as the agricultural editor on the *Decatur* (Ill.) *Herald*. That six-year stint followed by a similar two-year post on the *St. Louis Globe-Democrat* make her one of the pioneers, if not the first woman agricultural reporter on a major newspaper. Later, Jean became one of the better-known contributors to the *Herald of Holiness* and often wrote on assignment for children's Sunday School publications.

When her husband died from a lingering malignancy in the depth of the depression, Jean was left with two adult children, a 13-year-old daughter, and a small widow's pension. Fifteen years later, that daughter's violent act filled her cup of sorrow with undiluted grief.

The spiritual strength to survive the shock came from a member of the family into which she had been adopted in 1934—her Heavenly Father. Jean became a Christian at the altar of the Church of the Nazarene in Ontario, Calif. The saving grace and sanctifying power she experienced at that place of prayer enabled her to mature as a believer. Hers was a preparation for a fateful Sunday afternoon she did not know was in her future.

Jean's younger daughter becomes the focus of the story at this point. Married at 17 to a Christian naval officer whom she had met at church, it could have been a happy union.

But it wasn't.

Neither her compassionate husband nor the two children who later came to grace their home were able to interrupt the cycle of boredom and depression. On several occasions, across the years, despair led to attempted suicide. The usual pattern was for her to overdose on sleeping pills when she was alone in a remote hotel room.

Only the combination of good fortune and medical skill had kept her alive. She became a common figure, and a model patient, at the state mental hospital in San Bernardino, Calif.

During the year when her son was 10 and her daughter was 7, the young mother seemed on her way to complete healing. Thanksgiving Day was an extremely happy occasion in their San Diego home. Just a bit more than 24 hours later, a Los Angeles hospital called. Jean's daughter had just been admitted, victim of an overdose, having been discovered in a comatose state in an inexpensive hotel room in downtown L.A. When she had recovered, she was readmitted to the state hospital for further therapy.

The following March, when she was permitted total freedom, she left the hospital one Sunday afternoon. Three hours and seven miles later she threw herself off an overpass and died instantly from a broken neck.

Now, many years later, Jean Leathers Phillips remembers her troubled daughter. Clearly Jean's writing skills have not diminished as she shares the story in her own words.

> Mid-spring and a warm, sunny, blossom-scented morning gave no intimation of tragic news in the offing. Waiting correspondence had been shuffled and restacked on the study desk twice or more. A scripture, long known and loved, began running through my thinking:
>
> *Fear not: for I have redeemed thee, I have called thee by thy name; thou art mine. When thou passest through the waters, I will be with thee; and through the rivers, they shall not overflow thee: when thou walkest through the fire, thou shalt not be burned; neither shall the flame kindle upon thee* (Isa. 43:1-2).
>
> Somehow it was borne into my thinking that the prophet hadn't recorded "if," but had written "when." In the midst of this thought my son-in-law came. My

daughter, his wife, and the mother of their two young children had accomplished self-destruction on her sixth try.

My son-in-law broke the sad information as gently as he knew how. My response was unexpected, and surprising to some people. As I look back, I can see that my calmness came from an event which had taken place 10½ months earlier while my daughter lay at the point of death in a Los Angeles hospital. I released her totally to the Lord. I surrendered her so completely that for the last year of her earthly life she was no longer mine.

Our pastor and many, many friends surrounded us and supported us as soon as the news became known. I cannot explain it, except to believe that it was part of God's healing touch—nearly every sympathy card contained those verses from Isaiah 43.

I saw nothing spectacular—heard no "voices." There was just a calm confidence that the Lord had allowed what was best for all concerned. I could not argue nor doubt His judgment. He was present and tenderly held in His keeping all that I had committed to Him months earlier.

My daughter's hopeful testimony at church a few months before her death is still a stay to me these 20 years afterward. I feel an assurance and have, from time to time, that she was not mentally responsible. I believe that mental illness is as real as physical illness. There will be a reunion. I am confident she is with the Lord—"Lost a while, then found forever."

The Lord's preparation and sustaining grace has been mine in many dark places. In every situation I have had the light of His loving-kindness out before me, and I am confident it will be there—always. For that reason, in my middle 80s, I pray, serve, and continually keep an upward look.

For Jean Phillips, the greatest challenge to her faith came after years of crisis. While no one can ever completely prepare for this kind of crushing sorrow, God had been graciously molding her life for months.

On other occasions in human experience, we are required to make life-changing decisions without warning and minus the luxury of a quiet time to consider the consequences. That is the focus of our story in the next chapter. It relates what happened shortly after an airplane landed one day in Charlotte, N.C.

6

The Unplanned Response to a Crisis

Okie peered anxiously out the window of the Delta Air Lines passenger jet as it landed at the airport in Charlotte, N.C.

Everything looked strange. But then, she had not expected to recognize anything. She was half a world away from the country of her birth. Never before in her 23 years had she travelled outside her Korean homeland. International air travel was an impossible dream, not an occasional luxury for Korean families like hers.

But here she was. As the children used to shout when they played hide-and-seek, "Here I am, ready or not!"

Along with the other passengers, Okie hustled out of the plane into the airport lobby. Caught in the crush of family reunions and businessmen meeting clients, she could not see if there was someone there to greet her. The "big" Americans seemed to engulf her. Like most of her countrymen, Okie is small. Actually, smaller than most, she is a tiny 4 feet 8 inches in height.

The tiny Korean traveller moved to the edge of the crowd. Her eyes darted from face to face. There was no need to try and read the signs. That was impossible. She did not understand English. She was confident, however, that the one American she knew, would be there. She had met him in Korea. He had promised to love her "till death do us part."

Surely her soldier husband was in the milling crowd—somewhere. Okie kept looking. When the crowd thinned out, she walked to one end of the terminal, then to the other. Always looking—hoping to see that one friendly face.

But they were all strangers—all busy. Every one of them was speaking some language that had such funny sounds.

Okie returned to the gate where she had exited the plane. The lobby was empty. Only an occasional person walked quickly past toward an unknotn nation.

She sat down. Gradually it dawned on her that her husband was not going to meet her.

Anxiety was replaced with fear. Now what would she do?

She waited and thought and might have cried if she hadn't been so tired. Okie had been travelling nonstop for almost 24 hours.

Bill Tate was on duty as ground supervisor for Delta Air Lines in Charlotte when Okie's plane landed. An airlines supervisor has a major responsibility while a plane is on the ground. The needs of the plane, its cargo, and its passengers are all referred to him.

Especially the difficult and insoluble problems.

Thus it was that Bill learned about a war bride named Okie. But when he met her, he did not know that she was expecting to meet her soldier husband. Her passport simply identified her as a Korean. It was immediately evident that she spoke no English. Since neither he nor anyone else in the terminal knew Okie's native tongue, communication was nearly impossible.

During his years as a supervisor with Delta, Bill had encountered every conceivable emergency. He knew where to turn for immediate help and long-range assistance. He often took advantage of those social services designed to aid weary travellers. On many occasions he had referred confused or troubled passengers to them. They were caring people, but usually very busy. Without weighing the immediate cost or long-term implications, Bill made a quick decision that was in keeping with his Christian faith. He knew that he could not go to his comfortable home at the end of his shift and entrust Okie to an overworked welfare agency. She was too vulnerable—too alone.

When he made the decision to take her home for the night, he never doubted that his wife, Barbara, would respond just as he had. He was right, of course. Barbara urged him to bring Okie as quickly as possible. When Bill hung up the phone, he glanced at his desk calendar. The date was November 16, 1976.

Under different circumstances, Bill and Okie would have been a comical sight as they came through the door. Slender and tall at six feet four inches, Bill towered 20 inches above the slight little lady from the East.

But Barbara did not laugh, though she did manage a bit of a smile. The panic in Okie's face caught her attention.

"She just stood there . . . trembling. I looked into her eyes. They were filled with fear. She was so tired and so scared. I said, 'Hello,' but she didn't answer. I guess she just didn't know what the word meant."

Then Barbara did something that no man, regardless

of his efficiency or compassion, could do. She opened her arms and Okie ran to her.

Volumes of love were communicated by that tender touch. Okie knew that she had found a friend. But that was about all anyone knew at that moment. It would be days before they began to understand the story and weeks before the problem began to be resolved. It will take eternity to measure the wide-reaching implications of the experience.

It was immediately evident, however, that the Tates were woefully unprepared for the challenge of having this little Korean as their house guest. While Barbara waited for them to arrive from the airport, she decided she would prepare herself for the encounter. She turned in the encyclopedia to "Korea." Her primary concern was to cook some food that Okie would like. All it said was that Koreans ate lots of rice. It was weeks before she learned that Koreans prepare it much differently than she did for her family.

Customs, culture, food, language—these were just some of the challenges presented by their unexpected visitor.

Money was another factor. Bill had a good salary with Delta Air Lines. But he already had the needs of three children to meet: two teenagers, Steve and Beverly, and an active six-year-old named Scott.

There was another very obvious problem—Okie was 7½ months pregnant.

In fact, this is what had brought her on her flight into the unknown. Children with American GI fathers have no future in Korea. They have absolutely no civil rights. These mixed-race children cannot attend public school, are denied even the most menial jobs in a factory, cannot join the military, or even apply for employment with the government. They are outcasts.

Okie's pregnancy was complicated by yet another fact. International air lines have rules restricting the flight of expectant mothers after they reach their eighth month of pregnancy.

There had been some indications that her husband, Larry, planned to bring her to the United States as soon as he could work it out. Far away in Korea there was no way to know that Larry was doing his best, especially in light of the obstacles he had encountered when he returned home. No one among his family and friends looked with favor at the idea of a Korean war bride becoming a part of their community. Larry was discouraged. He was learning that these things take time.

But Okie could not wait.

No loving family wants their child to move hundreds of thousands of miles away with the full knowledge that they would never see them again. However, when they looked around and saw what was happening to the half-breed children on the streets, they knew they had no choice. Okie must go to America—immediately. If only they had the money.

An older sister came up with the answer. She and her husband had borrowed money to purchase a piece of property near Seoul. Without asking her husband for approval, she took Okie downtown to the office of Korean Air Lines. There they bought a ticket for Charlotte, North Carolina where Okie thought Larry was living.

But Larry was not there. He picked up his mail in a little town several hundred miles away, where his parents lived.

After Okie had been living with the Tates for some time, a reporter for the *Charlotte Observer* heard about the experience. His front page story recounted the details, giving special attention to the compassionate involvement of Bill and Barbara Tate. He said nothing about the extra financial pressure the family was feeling. However, his readers were able to read between the lines. Unsolicited offers of help began to flood the newspaper. Soon, Okie's needs were adequately met.

The people of Charlotte wanted to do far more than this, however. When they learned that the recently-discharged soldier had not been able to find employment, there were many job offers. A house was offered at low rent to aid the young couple. While these experiences of kindness kept coming, an aggressive reporter discovered where Larry was living. He was overwhelmed by the way the Charlotte community had rallied to help him and Okie. Thus it was that after many weeks, a frightened Korean war-bride was reunited with her husband. Together they began the tough task of building a happy home.

Fortunately, they were not alone. Bill and Barbara Tate and their children are all dedicated Christians. The little mother-to-be who had entered their life without warning had left quite an impact on them. They continued to be involved with Larry and Okie. Their nonaccusing acceptance made it easier for Larry to weather the notoriety and publicity. Larry and Okie became a part of their circle of friends. And for the Tates, that meant the church.

Bill and Barbara are happy activists in the Church of the Nazarene. At the present time, he is a lay member of the District Advisory Board and was one of the delegates from the North Carolina District to the recent General Assembly. In recent years, Barbara has become deeply involved in children's ministries, not only in the local church, but also in teachers' workshops throughout the area.

Yet, in spite of all their Christian involvement in outside projects, the Tates are primarily interested in their local church. They were pleasantly committed to the

Thomasboro Church of the Nazarene when it became clear that First Church in Charlotte was going through a period of intense crisis. Characteristically, when they were assured that it was the leading of the Lord, they left their comfortable church for hard work on the religious frontier.

The Tates were still attending the Thomasboro church when Okie arrived. It was a normal expression of their love and faith for them to invite the young couple to be a part of their Christian fellowship. Thus, a great many people shared the joy the Sunday Larry and Okie asked Jesus Christ to become the Lord of their lives.

The North Carolina Korean community responded with overflowing gratitude when the story became public. They could hardly believe that an unknown white couple would be so kind to a vulnerable Oriental. Later on, they invited the Tates to a special dinner.

"They treated us like royalty," Barbara remembers, "but we came back home to dirty dishes!" Ah yes, but you can always come home to dirty dishes for far less meaningful reasons.

Partly as a result of the new coverage, a Korean church was organized. The only "white American" dignitaries invited to the first service were Bill and Barbara Tate.

United Press International picked up the story and distributed it on its national news line. Soon the Tates were receiving letters of appreciation from a great many grateful Koreans, especially in the eastern United States. Even now, several years later, they receive Christmas cards from Koreans they have never met. Among them is a Christian Korean who lives in Cincinnati, Ohio, who phones occasionally just to keep in touch. The Tates have made a great many new friends.

Okie's family was delighted, also. When they finally learned what had happened, the sister wrote Barbara. It cost the sister $32.00 in U.S. money to have the letter translated into English and typed. "It was such a lovely letter," Barbara remembers happily.

But it was not all easy. There were also ugly letters, filled with hostility and prejudice. Not everyone approved the outflowing of love to a racially mixed couple. It was not easy to sleep at night after one of these messages of hate arrived.

There were many happy, and some quite humorous, experiences while Okie was living with the Tates. But at times it was emotionally exhausting. The pressure of the harsh letters and the drain of being compassionate was taking its toll.

"One night," Barbara recalls, "I had finally reached the end. I asked, *Lord, are we into something we can't get out of?*

"Within a few hours, the answer came. It became clear that this was not an unplanned event. It didn't just happen that Bill was on duty when Okie's plane arrived. She was in our home by appointment, not accident."

Barbara continues, "We have learned so much from being with Okie. Everyone in the family has learned to be more sensitive to the people who pass our way. We've learned that we are here under appointment to say something for the Lord. We'll never be the same. Nor do we want to be."

The passing of the years has caused the families to drift apart. They attend different churches now and live in widely separated parts of Charlotte. They see each other only occasionally, and perhaps that is the way it should be. It allows Larry and Okie to continue to grow. But the friendship continues. Just recently when Barbara answered the phone, Okie was on the other end of the line. Before their conversation was completed, Okie told her, "Mom, I pray every day, 'Make me a good woman.'"

Bill's unplanned response to a person in need resulted

in months of compassionate involvement and an ever-widening circle of ministry. It is a beautiful example of holy love in action.

The lonely and the disenfranchised face many challenges. It is not easy to be poor.

Financial success has its temptations, also. In the next chapter, we will meet a couple who were forced to come to grips with the opportunity to take the easy life at the cost of devotion to Jesus Christ. Readers will be pleased to learn the unexpected result.

7

Could a Man Ask for More?

There is a highly visible squadron of preachers abroad in the land who proclaim that it is God's will for every Christian to be healed—that is, if only we can find someone to "pray the prayer of faith." If that is not possible, they will gladly make their services available in exchange for a contribution to the support of their television program. Most of these preachers also trumpet the message that our Heavenly Father wants all of His children to travel first class. "After all," they argue, "God owns the cattle on a thousand hills . . . would He refuse to give any good thing to His faithful followers?"

If we believe that the currently popular "prosperity philosophy" is a valid expression of Christianity, we might not enjoy this chapter—simply because the central character has not always been successful by these standards.

In all honesty, it must be admitted, right here at the beginning, that if the quality of a man's faith is to be judged by his ability to always get what he wants through

58

prayer, then Robert Potbury's religion is suspect. However, before we allow that conclusion to be set in concrete, let us read the rest of the story.

Recently, Bob has faced some unusually difficult challenges. Two examples are illustrative:

Bob loves to fly and has been a private pilot for many years. Except for his devotion to his wife Bernardine and their family, and his commitment to Jesus Christ, he has no greater love in his life than flying. Nor did he pursue this hobby to escape from his wife. Flying has been a family affair. In fact, Bernardine recently shared this personal insight into their relationship: "One of the nicest things Bob ever did for me was to let me learn to fly."

Then, suddenly, Bob developed a serious heart problem. Unexpectedly, he could no longer pass the flight physical. When he was forced to turn in his pilot's license, he experienced one of the saddest days of his life. Not long after that came another terrible blow when he sold his airplane.

God had not answered Bob's prayer for healing. His pastor at the St. Marys, Ohio, Church of the Nazarene remembers how it affected Bob: "It crushed him! When he sold his plane, it was almost more than he could handle."

Unanswered prayer is incredibly difficult for anyone who believes that "God answers prayer." It is especially tough on those who, like Bob, have a daily devotional schedule which they rarely miss. Early each morning, he goes into the quiet family room to spend some time with the Lord. He prayed again and again for good health, and it was denied him.

About the same time he also asked the Lord whether or not he should sell his business. He confided with his pastor that it was "a handsome offer. If I sell out now, I can continue at my current standard of living and never work another day."

The sign advertising Bob's business reads, "Potbury Ford." He is a dealer in new and used cars. He has owned the Ford dealership in St. Marys since 1959.

Bob prayed about the unsolicited offer to sell his car dealership. Finally, it seemed to him that God did not want him to sell.

Within a few short months interest rates soared upward out of control, and the car business went sour. His "small-town car business," as he calls it, changed dramatically. He had been selling about 200 new cars and 250 used cars each year, generating about $2 million in sales and service.

He could have retired to a life of ease when he was abruptly faced with the need to work as hard as when he began.

It would seem to some that God had gone on vacation and disconnected the phone. Many people would have quit praying.

But not Bob. He quietly asked the Lord to help him diversify. Now he is selling almost enough used cars to overcome the shocking loss in new car sales.

Yet, these have been times of intense spiritual struggle. The combined loss of health and the business recession have been a heavy burden. Emotional and spiritual recovery were not automatic, but the healing has occurred.

One of the closest observers of the time of temptation and trial was Bob's pastor, John Williamson, who observes: "I watched him come back and marvel at how God has given him the courage and strength to make it through everything that has happened to him."

Thus his wife could say, even after this period of stress, "I feel that Bob is one of the few people that have seen his dreams come true. It has not always been easy, but Bob was so thoroughly convinced that God had sent us to St. Marys that we could never doubt for a moment that whatever came our way was in God's providence."

Bob adds, "Don't build it up that we're tremendously successful. We're not millionaires. We've just got a small-town car business. But the Lord's been good to us. We've had three meals a day and had a nice house to live in. My daughter was able to go through college—my son didn't want to go. Lots of people would look at us and say that we're not successful . . . but we've been happy."

How does a person come to enjoy that kind of mature Christian faith?

The route is different for everyone, but for Bob it began in a parsonage. His father was a pastor in the Free Methodist church for 44 years. His character development continued during the years he spent in the United States Navy during World War II. A big moment came when he was the best man at a friend's wedding in Flint, Mich. There he met the bride's sister.

Bob and Bernardine had their first date in the time between rehearsal and the wedding. She, too, was a preacher's kid. Her father was a minister in the Mennonite Brethren in Christ church.

The Flint Central Church of the Nazarene was the site of their wedding, more than 42 years ago. Bernardine had become a Christian when she was just five years of age. Bob did not make a life-changing commitment to Christ until after they were married.

Another major factor in Bob's spiritual development was the happy group of young married couples in the Detroit First Church of the Nazarene. They enjoyed each other, loved the Lord, and had great respect for their teacher, Harlan Heinmiller. His life was a continual witness to the grace of God while his infectious smile was the first step on the road to recovery from many a disappointment.

Yet, with all its joys, Bob was not immune to challenge and temptation. One incident from his younger days reveals how the harsh demands of life can both develop and reveal character.

Bob took a job as the parts manager for a successful car dealer in Detroit. He remembers them having been very kind to him; and "as businessmen go, they were exceptionally honest." They treated their customers and employees well but became incensed when they were cheated. On those rare occasions they would do anything to recover their loss.

One day, the story circulated through the shop that the owners had lost a lot of money on a "fast deal." Joe, one of the owners, came to Bob and said, "I want you to write up some warranty orders so we can get money back from Chevrolet to pay what that fellow stole from us."

"Joe," Bob replied, "I can't do that."

Joe responded, "That's a direct order. You have to do it!"

"No, it's not honest, I won't do it."

"This could have very serious implications, if you don't follow orders," Joe threatened. Then he added as he left, "Think about it carefully, and I'll see you in 30 minutes."

Bob thought about it. People in management at that dealership worked for very low wages. At the end of the year they were compensated with large bonuses, "to set everything right." It was mid-November. Bob wondered how his decision would affect his bonus—or his job. His girl was about three years old; his boy had not yet been born. He had a family to support. In addition, he had just made a big pledge on the church's building program.

Bob recalls what happened next: "I don't think it was 29 minutes or 31 minutes. At exactly 30 minutes I heard my name on the intercom telling me to go to the owner's office. When I entered, I could tell that he had cooled down quite a bit."

In brief, their conversation went like this:

"Bob, I know you've thought this over; haven't you? I want you to go ahead and do as I tell you."

"Joe, I can't. If I would steal for you, I would steal from you, and I'm not going to do either."

In great anger the boss shouted, "Get out of here!"

Bob expected to be fired. Instead, at the end of that year he was given the largest bonus he ever received from that company.

Several years later, when Bob was the acting general manager, it became clear to him that there would be no more advancements with that dealership. He submitted his resignation.

One morning at his devotions, a surprising event took place. "That morning," Bob recalls, "I thought I heard an audible voice saying, 'Ask largely, that your joy might be full.'

"It kinda shocked me. I was stunned for a minute. Then I prayed, *Lord, if that's it, then I'm going to ask real big. I don't want a job; I want my own business.*

"I went upstairs and woke up my wife and told her, 'Bernie, we're not looking for any more jobs, we're going into the car business!' "

More swiftly than he could imagine, Bob Potbury was offered the Ford dealership in St. Marys, Ohio. His answer to prayer was at a location where the five previous dealers had gone bankrupt.

But Bob worked hard and God worked miracles.

One early morning he prayed, *Lord, would You please help me sell some used cars today. It's really important, Lord, because I have all my money tied up in them, and I couldn't sell a new car unless the customer paid cash.*

Three days later he prayed, *Lord, would You please help me sell some new cars; I don't have any used cars left!*

From a business perspective, the move to St. Marys was attractive and exciting. It was the fulfillment of a dream.

Their initial experience with the church was exactly the opposite. This is not to imply that the St. Marys church was deficient or inferior to their home church in Detroit. But it was different! The Potburys were city folk, accustomed to the wide variety of programs and social opportunities a large church can provide.

The St. Marys Church of the Nazarene was small and rural in outlook. Neither understood the other, and mutual suspicion was the result.

Bob and Bernardine went "church shopping." They found several churches who courted them vigorously. It was clear that they thought that an aggressive young businessman would be a great asset to their congregation. From a cultural and social point of view, the Potburys were flattered. They discovered that the church world provided several attractive options.

In the end, the choice was made in relation to their two small children, Debbie and Don. Bob and Bernardine decided that it was worth whatever personal sacrifice they might have to make in order that their children would receive proper religious instruction. It was a decision they have never regretted.

Gradually, St. Marys became home; and, at the same time, the church people discovered that city folk and country folk are really not so different after all.

Six years after they arrived in St. Marys, the pastor asked Bob to become the chairman of the building committee. "Pastor," Bob replied, "I'll do anything, but not that. I've never built anything in my life."

That was true, but it was not the whole story. Bob was

plagued by a competing demand on his time. The building that housed his business was in terrible condition. He desperately needed to relocate and saw no way he could sell cars, build a church, and move his business—all at the same time.

One Sunday afternoon, Bob was in his office downtown "having a conference with the Chairman of the Board." Often, Bob would hold a private sabbath prayer meeting in the old building.

Lord, You know I'm willing to do anything, but I've never built anything in my life.

Does 'anything' include being chairman of the building committee?

Finally, after a struggle, Bob agreed: *Yes, Lord, it does. If You want me to be chairman, and the church wants me, I'll do my best. I desperately need a new building, but I am willing to wait until our new sanctuary is finished before I relocate.*

A week later, a local merchant with whom Bob had never done business made a "too good to resist" unexpected offer for his land and buildings. To his surprise and joy, Bob simultaneously supervised the construction of two new buildings. In front of one they placed a sign that read, "Church of the Nazarene"; the other sign announced, "New Home of Potbury Ford."

And his business was never better!

Several years later when the church built a Christian Family Life Center, Bob was one of the laymen who made the project possible. During the tough, later days of construction, Bob kept encouraging the pastor with the motto, "The faint heart never won the fair lady." That may be the most unusual "scripture" verse that ever brought a church building project to completion.

This is Bob's story, but he would quickly remind everyone that he is just one of a great group of faithful laymen in the St. Marys church. It is their dedicated spirit of happy cooperation that has made this the most optimistic era in the church's history.

Bob and Bernardine's two children are married: their daughter, Debbie, to Jim Gies; son Don, to Donna.

And they have "one really grand granddaughter named Laura."

"The biggest blessing," says Bob, "is that both of our kids, now grown and married, are in the church. Sometimes on Sunday morning I see my daughter at the piano, my wife in the choir, and, occasionally, my son singing in a quartet. The tears run right down my cheeks. I'm so glad."

Could a man ask for more?

Probably not.

However, many good people have made that same request and it was denied them. They exhibited Christ in the home, faithfully supported the church, and provided every opportunity for their children to choose the Lord's way.

But sometimes the intercessory prayers of Christian parents go unanswered. In the next chapter we will meet one of those parents, cry with her in her anguish, and rejoice in her victory.

8

Free to Love Again

In this chapter we find the terrifying collision between the moral values of a mother and those of her daughter. The words come directly from the mother. She is a real person. The story actually happened. However, to protect the love that is being renewed between mother and daughter, the names have been changed.

The details of this relationship are uniquely theirs. There are, unfortunately, thousands of Christian parents who are engulfed in a crisis of moral values between them and their teenage children. The circumstances differ, but the tension and the tragedy is just as real. May each of them be encouraged to believe that the Lord will also grant them peace.

The Fourth of July dawned a beautiful, warm day. Little did I dream that what I would learn that day would shatter me for years to come. It focused on our lovely teenage daughter. On that fateful morning, Kathy Ann was extremely restless. She would go outside, then come back inside. She made one phone call, then another. When I asked her what was wrong, she replied, "Oh, nothing"— then ran from my presence.

About noon, she came into the kitchen crying uncontrollably. I rushed to her, took her in my arms, and tried to find out what was wrong. She said she couldn't tell me—I wouldn't understand. Eventually, when she had calmed down a little, she decided to visit one of her girl friends with whom she graduated from high school. That gave me time to reflect on the past.

When Kathy Ann was nine months old, the Lord spoke to me about giving our four children to Him. Three times within several months, I had heard sermons on Abraham's offering his son as a sacrifice, in obedience to God. After the first two sermons, I clutched our babies close to me and cried out to God, *No—I can't give them up! I can't, I can't.*

When the third sermon was preached, I knew the time had come. I looked at dear Kathy Ann sleeping in my arms—perspiration causing her curly hair to form damp ringlets round her rosy face; then to our young son leaning on me from the adjoining seat with his blanket in his arms, sucking his thumb trying to keep awake; then just beyond him to our two older children and thought, *How can I do this? How, God?*

Finally, having made my decision, I asked a friend to hold my sleeping baby and rushed to the altar where I gave each to God by name. I was emotionally drained. But it was done! I had obeyed God. Little did I know then that this was to be the redeeming act that would keep my sanity many times in the years to come.

It proved to be the case again on that national holiday.

After Kathy Ann left, my husband asked me to go to the store with him. I agreed. Before leaving, I went into Kathy Ann's room, asking God to show me some way to help my dear, troubled daughter. On the bed, I saw an open letter. Hoping to get a clue, I picked it up. I had never before read my children's mail unless they shared it with me. But that day I was grasping for some way to help her.

The letter shocked me to agonizing disbelief. Written in my daughter's own hand, it revealed that she had been rejected by a girl friend with whom she wanted to have a sexual relationship. Kathy Ann was a lesbian.

My breathing almost stopped!

My husband called from the front room. Quickly, I put the letter back into the envelope and made my way through the door to the car where he was waiting. I was stunned to silence.

As we shopped in the nearly vacant store, all I could think of was, No! No! It can't be true! I can't even think it, let alone say it! Our lovely Kathy Ann a—a—a—*O God!*

In the process of shopping, my husband had gone ahead of me to the next aisle. I could hardly keep the tears from spilling down my face as I stood there all alone. I leaned against the brooms and mops, lifted my face to God, and whispered in anguish, *Where were You?*

The agony that pounded my mind was like the waves that crash again and again against the cliffs!

Where were You? Where were You? Didn't You see what was going on? I kept asking the questions. I thought I would surely die!

I heard my name. My husband was asking a question. I turned and headed mechanically toward him. My heart and head were pounding so much that I was sure I would never reach him if God did not intervene. It was then that I felt myself being wrapped in what I now know was His grace. As I turned the corner, my heart and mind stopped racing, and I was breathing normally again. It was almost as if I had awakened from a hallucination—that this was only a bad, bad dream!

But it was not a dream! It was a living nightmare. My life had been so sheltered, both as a child and as an adult that homosexuality was something that I seldom heard mentioned. It was just a word to me then. Now it was to be like the pendulum in the story of *The Pit and the Pendulum*—about to cut the very life out of me.

Because I was so ignorant and so desperately ashamed, I could not talk to anyone. Not even to my husband. At that time, he was ill and unable to work. I felt that our household could not handle two shattered people. I did not have the courage to confront her with what I had learned. Unable to cope with the news, I could not help her or anyone else. She moved out shortly afterwards.

For five years, I carried this unbearable burden. For five years, I made sure my mask was in place before going to church or anywhere else. When I overheard remarks about "this life-style," I was filled with condemnation and hatred. I felt like an accused criminal, about to be caught. I wanted to run away and hide! There were times when I would get out the map and try to locate a small town in our state, or a nearby state, and start making plans to run away, change my name, and never let anyone know where I was. But God stopped me. He and I both knew that this load of "black truth" would follow me.

Once I began to reveal my heartache to a Christian "friend"; but before the entire story came out, the comment was made, "Well, what did you expect?"

That remark sent me to the pits for months. I examined our home, how we had reared the children, and could find no reason for Kathy Ann's decison to become a lesbian. We took our children to church and Sunday School every Sunday, prayer meeting and youth activities every week. We failed in some areas, I know, but not to warrant "this"!

Where was the validity of the promise that was in the Word—"Train up a child in the way he should go: and when he is old, he will not depart from it" (Prov. 22:6)? This verse mocked me again and again!

At the end of this five-year period of intense distress, I came to the point that I told God, *Give me relief or else I'll die!*

In mercy, the Lord led me to a godly minister. I unloaded all my anguish and heartache, sorrow and disappointment, shame and despair on him. He was gracious, uncondemning, and compassionate. After the tears and words had subsided, he spoke directly from God's heart to mine. With words as tender as Christ must have spoken, he related to me of the situation of another family. The daughter had rebelled and finally left home. The grief-stricken parents were given this counsel by their pastor: "Give your daughter over to the Holy Spirit. Let Him be her Guide, her Protector, her Corrector, her Provider, her Keeper, and her Parents."

I do not remember all that he said. I only know that what he said would eventually set me free. Free to take off the mask—free to love again—free to live again!

I left the pastor's office that day feeling like "the fever had broken," and I was going to get well! When I reached home, I went into the bedroom, closed the door, fell facedown on the floor, and there I gave dear Kathy Ann to God. I thought of all the events of the five years since that dark Fourth of July and gave them all to the Holy Spirit. I do not know how long I lay there. When I got up, the commitment of Kathy Ann to God was complete. I fell across the bed exhausted.

That was the beginning of a new day in my life. Slowly but surely God healed all the deep wounds of the past. He showed me that the coat of guilt and shame I had been wearing had not been put there by Him. With this revelation, I came to the awareness that this coat had been thrown on me by myself and others. What it did was keep me from God and drive me almost to the point of insanity with despair. From that point on, the Holy Spirit helped me to shed this "Satan-colored coat"—and eventually released me.

As the months passed, I felt a marvelous thing happening to me. I was loving Kathy Ann in a new way—a freer way! Gone were the questionings such as, "How could you do this to yourself? How could you do this to us?" Gone were the feelings of ultimate doom for her. In their place was a special awareness of God. It was *His love* for Kathy Ann that was filling my heart! God was loving her through me!

Our relationship with Kathy Ann was never broken, though it was strained. She did not come around very much, but she knew the door was always open, and she knew that we loved her.

Many, many times during those five years, when I would get distressed almost beyond endurance, God would say to me, "Louisa, leave her to Me!" I had not been able to let her go mentally, emotionally, or spiritually. Now I could!

During the years since then, God has proven to me, again and again, how very much He does love her! She has gone through some very rough times. Illness, accidents, poverty. Through all these, God has told me, "Hands off! Remember, she is Mine now." I have been able to release her with the assurance that God was doing more than I could ever dream of doing. He was bringing Kathy Ann to himself, in His own way. That way is right. I can fully trust Him.

For some time she lived in a small commune in another part of the state. While she was living there, we visited her. It was a beautiful place. Not the buildings, they were huts; but the natural beauty was very inviting. Yet there was such an oppressive spirit that I could hardly wait to leave. As we departed, she followed us down the driveway and yelled, "I love you!"

It was as if we were climbing out of a pit, leaving our daughter there. The pull of love to us as we left was not strong enough to overcome the pull Satan had on her life, so she stayed. I cried for a long time as we headed home. From that "pit," I can still hear her call, "I love you!"

With all that the Lord had done, I still had difficulty feeling right about actively serving the Lord. Recently I told our pastor of Kathy Ann, and now about my hesitancy about working actively for the Lord. I felt "disqualified." He quoted to me the verse from Gen. 50:20: "You intended to harm me, but God intended it for good" (NIV). With those words, I now feel free to work actively for the Lord, and am doing so.

Once when Kathy Ann was visiting, she asked me what I thought of her life-style. I gently told her that I did not approve of it, neither did God. But I also told her that I loved her! And how God loved her!

It will soon be nine years since that dark discovery on that bright Fourth of July. I have gone "through the valley of the shadow of death" (Ps. 23:4). I have learned much; I still have much to learn. But this I do know: The love she has for us is a precious gift from heaven. It has withstood the fires of hell and purified the affection we had for each other before this.

Recently she sent me a card that said, "All roads lead back to you. I love you, Mom." I am on my way to heaven, and I know she will follow me—all the way.

This would be an appropriate moment to pause and pray for all the Kathy Anns in our world—those children who have rejected their Christian heritage and brought pain to themselves and their families.

It would also be timely to pause in gratitude for the servants of God who have taken the gospel message to remote places. As William Vaughters has said, "You never know where God is going to go to find His good ones." The next chapter about "Little Arnoldo" is such a story.

9

Little Arnoldo

The ragtag parade down the main street of Livingstone, Guatemala, hardly seemed to be the start of anything important.

But it was—especially for a boy named Arnoldo. The son of an American GI and a Mayan Indian, those few blocks were the start of a lifelong adventure for this young lad, an adventure of grander proportions than anyone could have imagined.

The parade had been organized by missionary William Vaughters to advertise the beginning of the Nazarene Sunday School in this Caribbean coastal town.

The coastal area in and around Livingstone was known as the "White Man's Graveyard"—not because of the violence of the people (they were a peaceable lot), but because of the high incidence of malaria and amoebic dysentery. Everyone advised the missionary not to move his young family into that medically dangerous area. But God's servant was compelled by a greater motive than physical health or personal well-being.

William Vaughters preceded his family to Livingstone, where he built a small church and a simple, but comfortable, home on the beachfront. Located on the Bay of Honduras, Livingstone is one of the most beautiful cities in the world. The Dolce River loops around the city, flowing out of a verdant jungle of coconut palms, breadfruit trees, and tropical vegetation.

The wood homes, often painted red or green, provided colorful shelter for about 3,000 people—a mixture of blacks and local Indians, including the Caribe, Kekchi, and Mayans. Only one street is paved—the cobblestone main street that ran up from the dock. It is one of the few cities in the Americas that has the mystique of Tahiti.

The human situation was not as attractive, however. The central government of Guatemala was attempting to help the people, but with little success. Few families encouraged their children to attend the government-staffed elementary schools. The high illiteracy rate contributed to a spirit of indolence and carelessness. The men worked as little as possible and drank as much as they could afford. Few people left the area to upgrade themselves. Those who remained died early. The life span was about 45 years.

White men rarely visited Livingstone and almost never took up residence there. Thus the people watched Vaughters with ill-concealed interest. His building efforts regularly attracted a large group of "sidewalk superintendents"—many of them children. No one showed more interest than "little Arnoldo." It was no surprise, then, that he carried a drum in the parade down Main Street that Saturday morning. He was also present for the very first Sunday School session the next day.

Nor did he miss many services from that day on. A few months later, Mrs. Frances Vaughters had the joy of helping Arnoldo become a Christian in her junior Sunday School class.

In the providence of God, Larry and Ruth Vaughters, the missionaries' children, were about the same age as Arnoldo. Arnoldo never knew his father. He had been stationed nearby during World War II. His mother was forced to support herself and her only child. As a result of this combination of circumstances, Arnoldo became "like a son" in the Vaughters home. Though he never met his father, Arnoldo felt that he was a bit special because of that North American connection. He was also proud of his Mayan Indian heritage and still carries his mother's family name, Izaguirre (pronounced *Eezah-gear-ee*).

He became "something special" to the Vaughterses, too. The upward lift of the gospel of Jesus Christ, his pride in his heritage, and the new vistas opened by his daily contacts with the Vaughterses—all these were factors in the building of a dream in the heart of a half-breed Indian boy. It was a dream only rarely dreamed by any resident of Livingstone. The jungle that encircled Livingstone eventually could no longer contain his spirit. He yearned to experience the world beyond, the exciting outside world from which had come soldiers and missionaries. Through the missionaries he came to know Christ as his Savior and also to understand the importance of getting an education.

Educational opportunities were very limited in Livingstone. Arnoldo Izaguirre was 17 years of age when he made the tough decision to go outside. He chose to attend the Nazarene Bible School in Coban, Guatemala, where he completed his schooling through the sixth grade.

In Coban, Arnoldo was an excellent student and developed into a respected Christian leader in spite of his youth. He worked hard, supported himself, and consistently made the scholastic honor roll.

Before long, Arnoldo began to reach out again. The spiritual and academic stimulation at Coban was invigorating. No longer did it seem enough to obtain his sixth grade diploma. There was so much more beyond that—if only he could open the doors. In order to obtain a high school education, he became the pastor of the Church of the Nazarene in Flores, which is located in the Peten region of northeast Guatemala. It was never Izaguirre's goal to become a preacher; and apparently for that reason, he never accepted any financial help from the missionaries while he was a student in Coban. During this interim period, however, he was very successful as a lay preacher.

Arnoldo began to dream an impossible dream. He set his hope and aspirations on the national university, the University of San Carlos in Guatemala City. It was a dream Arnoldo had no right to dream. The national university was extremely selective in its choice of new students. Usually, it took more than good grades to be accepted. It was almost always the private province of the privileged. Those young people fortunate enough to be born into the homes of the wealthy and the influential were most often chosen. A half-breed Indian boy from the malaria coast had little chance.

But young Izaguirre refused to be discouraged by the overwhelming odds against him. His personal drive to achieve success was reflected in his excellent grades. They made the difference. As an honor student of highest caliber, he was given favorable attention by the university. Technically, the University of San Carlos is open to all who qualify. Arnoldo qualified. When registered at the university, he was filled with many emotions and the yet-to-be-answered question as to whether he could meet the scholastic competition.

Arnoldo was not alone in his concern about his entrance into the University of San Carlos. The leaders of the Church of the Nazarene in Guatemala were also keenly interested in the outcome. Few young men in the church showed greater promise than he. No one wanted to deny him any opportunity. Yet, there was the unspoken worry lest, having been accepted, it would be the occasion for him to lose his way spiritually. The church has lost some of her brightest and most qualified sons this way.

When the word was received that Arnoldo had been accepted into the national university, the response was both delight and fear. They congratulated him on his outstanding and unexpected achievement. Their fears were based on the fact that he had been accepted as a student in the School of Economics.

For most Christians in North America, the knowledge that Arnoldo Izaguirre was to attend the School of Economics would have little emotional content. In the United States and Canada, economics is studied as an academic subject, much as one might learn about math or astronomy. It is just another subject in the curriculum.

In most Latin American countries, however, the School of Economics is an evangelistic agency for the political philosophy of Karl Marx. Mature church leaders asked quietly, "Will Arnoldo be able to resist the pressure? Will he be another casualty?"

If Arnoldo had these fears, he did not reveal them. Instead, he gave himself to his studies with a great burst of energy. Soon it became apparent that he was one of the most gifted students in the school. Before long he was rewarded with a government job on the National Planning Board.

The first major clue the church had in relation to Arnoldo's religious intentions came when a decision was made to organize a new church—a church for professional people. Missionary James Hudson recalls that three university students became the nucleus for that new congregation: a prelaw student, Mr. Yaxcal; a premed student, Alfredo San Jose; and an honor student in the

School of Economics—Arnoldo Izaguirre! The question was beginning to be answered. Incidentally, that church known as Vivibien Zone 5 has continued to grow across these intervening years until it is now one of our strongest churches in Guatemala City. Its growth has not been impeded, even though two new churches have been organized from among the members of that congregation.

Characteristically, Arnoldo began to dream again. Once again the borders could not contain him. This time he set his sights on a professorship at the University of San Carlos. By all normal means, this seemed a greater impossibility than the difficulty of being accepted as a student. Half-breed Mayans with American soldier fathers were not prime candidates for teaching positions. Knowledgeable observers would not have called that dream unlikely—they would have scoffed at him for even supposing he had a chance.

As Izaguirre neared graduation, it became evident that many people had been watching this young man from Livingstone. His Christian friends congratulated him; the university conferred a degree on him with the highest honors, and the government of Guatemala awarded him a scholarship to study philosophy in Brazil. One can only guess what the 17-year-old boy had hidden in his heart when he left that isolated coastal village to study in Coban. Clearly, however, even he could not have imagined that he would receive so many high honors.

But they were not as great as he was to receive when he returned from Brazil. His mentor, the rector of the School of Economics, offered him a professorship at the University of San Carlos.

Arnoldo's dream had come true.

A moment's interlude may be necessary to put this into perspective so that the significance of this opportunity is fully understood. Unlike North America,

Guatemala does not have a large middle class. Most of the people are relatively poor. A few are rich and influential. There is almost no upward movement. You are what you are born to be. Half-breed Indian boys from isolated fishing villages almost never rise above their heritage. The invitation to become a professor meant that Arnoldo Izaguirre could forever leave behind him the limitations of his poverty.

His dream had come true. Almost!

He was asked to teach two courses on the philosophy of Karl Marx. Here again, people living outside the Latin American culture can hardly understand what is involved in this opportunity. In North America, the philosophy of Karl Marx can be taught as an academic, secular subject. The teacher may be a Communist, but that is not necessary. He could just as easily be a Buddhist or a Christian.

But in Latin America the one who teaches such a class is expected to be an evangelist for Karl Marx and an exponent of international Communism.

"I'm sorry," Arnoldo Izaguirre said to the rector of the School of Economics, "but I cannot accept your gracious offer for me to teach the philosophy of Karl Marx."

The rector was dumbfounded. He could not imagine that anyone would turn down such a prestigious job, one that was sought by a great many people. Finally, he stammered, "Why?"

"Because I do not believe in the philosophy of Karl Marx."

"But you are a graduate of the School of Economics. Why don't you believe what you have been taught?"

"Because," Arnoldo responded quietly, "I am a Christian!"

"But you have to take it! And, besides, if you turn it down, you'll never get another chance."

"You are correct, I'm sure," Arnoldo agreed, "but I will not teach the philosophy of Karl Marx."

Izaguirre went back to his job on the National Planning Board. The dream faded!

As the years passed, Arnoldo married Estela de la Cruz, the daughter of one of the Nazarene pastors in Guatemala City. Their home has been blessed by three healthy, happy children, a son and two daughters. Slowly he received promotions on the job, gradually gaining a place of respect and authority.

But the choice had not been easy. Sometime later as he shared an evening meal with James Hudson, he revealed a bit of the struggle when he confided, "¡El diablo muy estuto!"—"The devil is very astute!"

Yes, the devil was astute, yet unable to successfully tempt Arnoldo to desert his faith.

But the final chapter had not been written. With his increased stature on the National Planning Board and a change in the administration at the School of Economics, the day eventually came when Arnoldo Izaguirre was asked, again, to become a professor at the university. Finally, in God's good time, and in keeping with his Christian convictions, Arnoldo's dream had come true.

Through it all he has stayed active in the church. Others in similar circumstances around the world have been grateful to the church but have made their friends among the intelligentsia.

Not Arnoldo.

One afternoon William Vaughters flew into Guatemala City to coordinate the church's ministry to the earthquake victims following the 1975 diaster. Izaguirre picked him up at the airport. After dinner, they went to a little church where Arnoldo was the lay preacher for a revival meeting. His sermon was a reflection of his faith: "one of the clearest and most beautiful messages on holiness I have ever heard," declared Vaughters. Then he added, "It is through men like him that we have a church in Guatemala."

In 1954, five years after he moved to Livingstone, Vaughters was forced to leave—seriously ill with malaria and amoebic dysentery.

"It really is the white man's graveyard," he now admits. "A person just has to obey and not know why some things come to you physically. Yet, God had a reason behind all of it. As we look at the fruit today, we see the reason. Actually, they carry on far better now than we ever could."

Then he concluded, "You never know where God is going to go to pick His good ones!"

A Final Thought

Our church does not confer sainthood on anyone—living or dead. The people we have met in the pages of this book are not saints in the sense that they have achieved the ultimate perfection attained by those who have received their final reward.

They are saints, however, in the highest and best New Testament definition of the term—saints in Christ Jesus. They are blood brothers to all those whose faith has been severely tested, who have felt the powerful pressure to fail, and yet have succeeded. They are part of that grand company who have lived for Christ in tumultuous times. Paul recognized that there were even saints "of Caesar's household" (Phil. 4:22).

These, the quiet in the land, have never asked for much, nor have they had all their prayers answered. Many of them could have lived more comfortable lives if they had chosen the ways of the world.

But they did not. Instead, they have received and given one great gift—God's peace and hope to a troubled world.

Bibliography

Cagle, Mary Lee. *Life and Work of Mary Lee Cagle: An Autobiography.* Kansas City: Nazarene Publishing House, 1928.

Hudson, Oscar. *This I Remember.* Kansas City: Beacon Hill Press of Kansas City, 1965.